This Is My Post Office

Adam Bellamy

Enslow Publishing
101 W. 23rd Street
Suite 240
New York, NY 10011
USA
enslow.com

Published in 2017 by Enslow Publishing, LLC.
101 W. 23rd Street, Suite 240, New York, NY 10011

Library of Congress Cataloguing-in-Publication Data
Names: Bellamy, Adam, author.
Title: This is my post office / Adam Bellamy.
Description: New York, NY : Enslow Publishing, LLC, [2017] | Series: All about my world | Audience:
Ages 5 up. | Audience: Pre-school, excluding K. | Includes bibliographical references and index.
Identifiers: LCCN 2016022718| ISBN 9780766081048 (library bound) | ISBN 9780766081024 (pbk.) |
ISBN 9780766081031 (6-pack)
Subjects: LCSH: Postal service—Juvenile literature.
Classification: LCC HE6078 .B35 2017 | DDC 383/.42—dc23
LC record available at https://lccn.loc.gov/2016022718

Printed in the United States of America

To Our Readers: We have done our best to make sure all websites in this book were active and
appropriate when we went to press. However, the author and the publisher have no control over and
assume no liability for the material available on those websites or on any websites they may link to.
Any comments or suggestions can be sent by e-mail to customerservice@enslow.com.

Photo Credits: Cover, p. 1 Tanya Little/Moment/Getty Images; peiyang/Shutterstock.com (globe icon
on spine); pp. 3 (left), 8 RJ Sangosti/Denver Post/Getty Images; pp. 3 (center), 16. Bob Berg/Moment
Mobile/Getty Images; pp. 3 (right), 14 © iStockphoto.com/DNY59; pp. 4–5 Ken Wolter/Shutterstock.
com; p. 6 Chris Hondros/Getty Images; p. 10 © iStockphoto.com/FredFroese; p. 12 © iStockphoto.
com/Juanmonino;. 18 Joe Raedle/Getty Images; p. 20 Boston Globe/Getty Images; p. 22 Cheryl Casey/
Shutterstock.com.

Contents

Words to Know 3

My Post Office 5

Read More 24

Websites 24

Index 24

Words to Know

package

post office box

stamp

United States
Post Office

UNITED

PARKING
VEHICLE ID
REQUIRED
UP TO $200 FINE
FOR VIOLATION

4

Main Post Office
Stillwater, MN

This is my post office.

STATES POST OFFICE

Main Post Office
St¨llwater, MN

Full Service Hours:
Mon. - Fri.   8:30am - 5:00pm
Saturday   10:00am - 12:00pm
Sunday & Holidays   Closed

Full Service Hours:
n 24 Hours Per Day/7 Days A Week

LIMITED EDITION
STAMPS

Many people visit the post office every day. They stand in line.

Some people need to send packages.

Some people need to send letters.

Some people need to buy stamps. There are many different kinds of stamps.

I have to put a stamp on my letter before I mail it.

Some people do not get their mail at home. They need to check their mail at a post office box.

Postal workers make sure packages arrive safely. They drive mail trucks.

Postal workers deliver mail to your home. They pick up that mail from the post office.

Going to the post office can be fun!

Read More

Kawa, Katie. *My First Trip to the Post Office*. New York, NY: Gareth Stevens Publishing, 2012.

Keogh, Josie. *A Trip to the Post Office*. New York, NY: PowerKids Press, 2012.

Loewen, Nancy. *Sincerely Yours: Writing Your Own Letter*. Mankato, MN: Picture Window Books, 2009.

Websites

American Historama

www.american-historama.org/1790-1800-new-nation/post-office.htm
Read about the history of the US Post Office.

Knowledge Adventure

www.knowledgeadventure.com/games/the-post-office//
Play a post office game..

Index

letters, 11

mail trucks, 19

packages, 9, 19

postal workers, 19, 21

post office box, 17

stamp, 13, 15

Guided Reading Level: B
Guided Reading Leveling System is based on the guidelines recommended by Fountas and Pinnell.

Word Count: 110